Fourtee[...] about

ex libris

Candlestick Press

Published by:
Candlestick Press,
Diversity House, 72 Nottingham Road, Arnold, Nottingham NG5 6LF
www.candlestickpress.co.uk

Design and typesetting by Craig Twigg

Printed by Bayliss Printing Company Ltd of Worksop, UK

Selection © Di Slaney and Katharine Towers, 2024

Cover illustration © Sara Boccaccini Meadows, 2024

Candlestick Press monogram © Barbara Shaw, 2008

© Candlestick Press, 2024

ISBN 978 1 913627 35 5

Acknowledgements

The poems in this pamphlet are reprinted from the following books, all by
permission of the publishers listed unless stated otherwise. Every effort has been
made to trace the copyright holders of the poems published in this book. The
editor and publisher apologise if any material has been included without
permission, or without the appropriate acknowledgement, and would be glad to
be told of anyone who has not been consulted.

Thanks are due to all the copyright holders cited below for their kind permission.

Kim Addonizio, *What is this Thing Called Love: Poems* (WW Norton, 2004)
copyright © 2004 by Kim Addonizio. Used by permission of WW Norton &
Company, Inc. Marjorie Allen Seiffert, *A Woman of Thirty and the Poems of Elijah
Hay* (Kessinger Publishing, LLC., 2010) in public domain. Hattie Grünewald,
https://poetrysociety.org.uk/poems/kiss/ and first published in this pamphlet by
kind permission of the poet. Roddy Lumsden, *Terrific Melancholy* (Bloodaxe
Books, 2011) www.bloodaxebooks.com. David Mills, *Boneyarn* (Ashland Poetry
Press, 2021). Shazea Quraishi, *The Art of Scratching* (Bloodaxe Books, 2015)
www.bloodaxebooks.com. Mary Ruefle, *Tristimania*, copyright © 2004 by Mary
Ruefle. Reprinted with the permission of The Permissions Company, Inc. on
behalf of Carnegie Mellon University Press, www.cmu.edu/universitypress.
Roberta Spear, *A Sweetness Rising: New & Collected Poems,* ed. Philip Levine
(Heyday Books, 2007) untraceable. Jean Toomer, *The Collected Poems of Jean
Toomer* (University of North Carolina Press, 1988) in public domain.

All permissions cleared courtesy of Dr Suzanne Fairless-Aitken –
Swift Permissions swiftpermissions@gmail.com

Where poets are no longer living, their dates are given.

Dream-Kiss

Moment of delight – most delicate,
Cool as a rose is cool;
Swift and silent as a pool
To mirror wings in flight;
Passionate as frost is passionate
With patterns intricate and white;
Pure as music in the night,
Far off, yet intimate –
It came
Poignant as beauty on swift feet of flame.
It paused… was gone… most delicate
Moment of delight.

Marjorie Allen Seiffert (1885 – 1970)

First time he kissed me, he but only kiss'd

First time he kissed me, he but only kiss'd
  The fingers of this hand wherewith I write;
  And ever since, it grew more clean and white,
Slow to world-greetings, quick with its "Oh, list,"
When the angels speak. A ring of amethyst
  I could not wear here, plainer to my sight,
  Than that first kiss. The second pass'd in height
The first, and sought the forehead, and half miss'd,
Half falling on the hair. O beyond meed!
  That was the chrism of love, which love's own crown,
With sanctifying sweetness, did precede.
  The third upon my lips was folded down
In perfect, purple state; since when, indeed,
  I have been proud, and said, "My love, my own!"

Elizabeth Barrett Browning (1806 – 1861)

Stolen Moments

What happened, happened once. So now it's best
in memory – an orange he sliced: the skin
unbroken, then the knife, the chilled wedge
lifted to my mouth, his mouth, the thin
membrane between us, the exquisite orange,
tongue, orange, my nakedness and his,
the way he pushed me up against the fridge –
Now I get to feel his hands again, the kiss
that didn't last, but sent some neural twin
flashing wildly through the cortex. Love's
merciless, the way it travels in
and keeps emitting light. Beside the stove
we ate an orange. And there were purple flowers
on the table. And we still had hours.

Kim Addonizio

Kiss

tarmac and dark grey cement flowed over her skin
and her hair was the colour of street lights
and when he looked at her,
the cars rushing past seemed only to be going
at 60 miles a decade.

her mouth tasted of newsagents when he kissed it
her lips smudged his.
eyes like rusty metal,
he kissed her.

and she didn't understand half the words he said
but she liked the feel of fabric softener
on her naked skin as she pulled off his shirt.
she liked the smell of expensive aftershave
and she reminded him of bubblegum machines
in fairgrounds.

their hearts were covered in grass stains;
the mud of trampled feet in the corner of a city park
when stars aren't visible under city smog
and the moon seems too old to care.

she could not even spell his surname
but when she danced she danced dark and
she was no longer lit by neon,
her skin no longer uncovered in public bathrooms
and he was traversing unknown territory
when she let him wander through her memories.
when he kissed her, he kissed privileged.

she spoke in plurals
and he breathed the words from her mouth
and smoke from her cigarette
and wine from her own breath.
her hands wander through the grass
to find her jeans' pocket
to pick up a mobile to talk to a friend
he watches her, without moving.

and oh, what loves these be,
overlooked by tired moon and old trees
and the scream of rough kids far away
skin rough, soul rough
but his touch smoothes it away
and his chest is like marble in a Parisian museum.
his eyes are silver coins
and he kisses by the public school book.

Hattie Grünewald

The Kiss

Before you kissed me only winds of heaven
    Had kissed me, and the tenderness of rain—
Now you have come, how can I care for kisses
    Like theirs again?

I sought the sea, she sent her winds to meet me,
    They surged about me singing of the south—
I turned my head away to keep still holy
    Your kiss upon my mouth.

And swift sweet rains of shining April weather
    Found not my lips where living kisses are;
I bowed my head lest they put out my glory
    As rain puts out a star.

I am my love's and he is mine forever,
    Sealed with a seal and safe forevermore—
Think you that I could let a beggar enter
    Where a king stood before?

Sara Teasdale (1884 – 1933)

Ae Fond Kiss

Ae fond kiss, and then we sever;
Ae fareweel, alas, for ever!
Deep in heart-wrung tears I'll pledge thee,
Warring sighs and groans I'll wage thee!

Who shall say that Fortune grieves him
While the star of hope she leaves him?
Me, nae cheerfu' twinkle lights me,
Dark despair around benights me.

I'll ne'er blame my partial fancy;
Naething could resist my Nancy;
But to see her was to love her,
Love but her, and love for ever.

Had we never loved sae kindly,
Had we never loved sae blindly,
Never met — or never parted,
We had ne'er been broken-hearted.

Fare thee weel, thou first and fairest!
Fare thee weel, thou best and dearest!
Thine be ilka joy and treasure,
Peace, enjoyment, love, and pleasure!

Ae fond kiss, and then we sever!
Ae fareweel, alas, for ever!
Deep in heart-wrung tears I'll pledge thee,
Warring sighs and groans I'll wage thee.

Robert Burns (1759 – 1796)

Why I Am Not A Good Kisser

Because I open my mouth too wide
Trying to take in the curtains behind us
And everything outside the window
Except the little black dog
Who does not like me
So at the last moment I shut my mouth.

Because Cipriano de Rore was not thinking
When he wrote his sacred and profane motets
Or there would be only one kind
And this affects my lips in terrible ways.

Because at the last minute I see a lemon
Sitting on a gravestone and that is a thing, a thing
That would appear impossible, and the kiss
Is already concluded in its entirety.

Because I learned everything about the beautiful
In a guide to the weather by Borin Van Loon, so
The nature of lenticular clouds and anticyclones
And several other things dovetail in my mind
& at once it strikes me what quality goes to form
A Good Kisser, especially at this moment, & which you
Possess so enormously – I mean when a man is capable
Of being in uncertainties, Mysteries & doubts without me
I am dreadfully afraid he will slip away
While my kiss is trying to think what to do.

Because I think you will try and read what is written
On my tongue and this causes me to interrupt with questions:
A red frock? Red stockings? And the rooster dead? Dead of what?

Because of that other woman inside me who knows
How the red skirt and red stockings came into my mouth
But persists with the annoying questions
Leading to her genuine ignorance.

Because just when our teeth are ready to hide
I become a quisling and forget the election results
And industrial secrets leading to the manufacture
Of woolen ice cream cones, changing the futures
Of ice worms everywhere.

Can it be that even the greatest Kisser ever arrived
At his goal without putting aside numerous objections –

Because every kiss is like throwing a pair of doll eyes
Into the air and trying to follow them with your own –

However it may be, *O for a life of Kisses*
Instead of painting volcanoes!

Even if my kiss is like a paintbrush made from hairs.
Even if my kiss is squawroot, which is a scaly herb
Of the broomrape family parasitic on oaks.
Even if a sailor went to sea in me
To see what he could see in me
And all that he could see in me
Was the bottom of the deep dark sea in me.
Even though I know nothing can be gained by running
Screaming into the night, into the night like a mouth,
Into the mouth like a velvet movie theatre
With planets painted on its ceiling
Where you will find me, your pod mate,
In some kind of beautiful trouble
Over moccasin stitch #3,
Which is required for my release.

Mary Ruefle

Interface

a kiss appears in the air
   within a room
or as a button at the neck
    of one known

which buttons one night
to its morning   where
we talk between love
   where   soft

in the light's spilldown
    a kiss is all
but talk   and spills
all   spilled

lightly into the pulse
    radar concision
the concealed heat
   hoaxed   raised

    from its lair
light heat   and pulse
risen in the notch
    between heads

a kiss appears   is air
   endures not as we wish
    as heat in the head
but as light

in the room we lay in
    as light as down
on one known skin
   endures *as wish* *within*

Roddy Lumsden (1966 – 2020)

Syllables and Lipstick

Your lips two pillows where my dreams rest.
Where do conversations end and kisses begin
when syllables and lipstick wear the same breath?

My dreams are six seas where I'm seldom wet.
Your breast: black bass swimming in your skin.
Your lips: two pillows where my dreams rest.

Sometimes silence has gotten up and left
when our mouths were crowded with sin,
since syllables and lipstick wear the same breath.

At night when the moon's an uninvited guest,
and your curtains become a womb for the wind,
your lips are two pillows where my dreams rest.

At daybreak most stars tend to speak of death
as the sun cracks the light in their ribs.
Now syllables and sunshine share the same breath.

Our tongues are the ways our mouths confess
to the voluptuous trouble we're in.
Your lips are two pillows where my dreams rest,
where syllables and lipstick wear the same breath.

David Mills

Her Lips Are Copper Wire

whisper of yellow globes
gleaming on lamp-posts that sway
like bootleg licker drinkers in the fog

and let your breath be moist against me
like bright beads on yellow globes

telephone the power-house
that the main wires are insulate

(her words play softly up and down
dewy corridors of billboards)

then with your tongue remove the tape
and press your lips to mine
till they are incandescent

Jean Toomer (1894 – 1967)

The Kiss

I go to close the shutters on a night
that will not darken or silence itself.
Wine glasses, bell chimes, street sweepers
go on singing without me.
Stooped in the shadows, a man gazes up
at me from his bench on the piazza
and blows me a kiss.
Suddenly, a bird swoops down and
scours the ground under the empty cafe tables.
Perhaps, a dove from the countryside.
Perhaps, a sign of his death or
mine. But the streetlamp blossoms
on the paving stones and no one
can see that the kiss has risen.
Risen not to the heavens, but
as close as you can get from here –
the third floor of No. 26 della Rotunda
where it slips through the thick
wooden slats and, with the kindness
of a stranger, enters my room.

Roberta Spear (1948 – 2003)

Sukumarika
to Ramasena

My dearest, my life,
moon to my night,
remember our happiness?

Recall, if you can,
the equal kiss, *Sama*,
and the pressed kiss, *Pidita*.
Aschita, the devouring kiss
and *Mridu*, the delicate kiss...
Also, the inflamer,
the kiss of encouragement,
the awakening kiss,
the vagabond, the joyful
kiss, the vibrant one,
the bowed kiss, the twisted kiss and
the satisfied kiss.

Have you forgotten
the taste of my mouth
sweetened with betel?
My garments, outer and inner,
white as milk.
The sound of my bangles
during love, their silence
in sleep.

Remember my lips
nibbling,
pinching,
kissing,
browsing,
sucking the mango,
devouring.

Remember
the way I make you feel – like twenty men –
and in your hands
my painted feet.

Shazea Quraishi

Kisses in the Train

I saw the midlands
　Revolve through her hair;
The fields of autumn
　Stretching bare,
And sheep on the pasture
　Tossed back in a scare.

And still as ever
　The world went round,
My mouth on her pulsing
　Throat was found,
And my breast to her beating
　Breast was bound.

But my heart at the centre
　Of all, in a swound
Was still as a pivot,
　As all the ground
On its prowling orbit
　Shifted round.

And still in my nostrils
　The scent of her flesh;
And still my blind face
　Sought her afresh;
And still one pulse
　Through the world did thresh.

And the world all whirling
　Round in joy
Like the dance of a dervish
　Did destroy
My sense – and reason
　Spun like a toy.

But firm at the centre
  My heart was found;
My own to her perfect
  Heartbeat bound,
Like a magnet's keeper
  Closing the round.

DH Lawrence (1885 – 1930)

Kisses Desired

Though I with strange desire
To kiss those rosy lips am set on fire,
Yet will I cease to crave
Sweet touches in such store,
As he who long before
From Lesbia them in thousands did receive.
Heart mine, but once me kiss,
And I by that sweet bliss
Even swear to cease you to importune more;
Poor one no number is;
Another word of me ye shall not hear
After one kiss, but still one kiss, my dear.

William Drummond of Hawthornden (1585 – 1649)